Peter Pfarl

SALZKAMMERGUT

130 Colour illustrations

BONECHI VERLAG STYRIA

Vertrieb
für Österreich
VERLAG STYRIA
Schönaugasse 64
A-8010 GRAZ

für Deutschland
AZN
Hooge Weg 71
D-47623 Kevelaer

für die Schweiz
Herder AG Basel
Muttenzerstraße 109
CH-4133 Pratteln 1

CONTENTS

© Copyright by Casa Editrice Bonechi - Florence - Italy
E-mail:bonechi@bonechi.it - Internet:www.bonechi.it

Printed in Italy by Centro Stampa Editoriale Bonechi

Photos taken by Luigi Di Giovine

Translation by Evelin Gwinner *for* Studio COMUNICARE, Florence

ISBN 3-222-11765-9

* * *

INTRODUCTION

Whereas today «Salzkammergut» evokes mountains, lakes and vacations, its name dates back to the time when the imperial officials so-identified the part of Austria from which salt came and which was directly dependent on the Court- and Finance Administration. Indeed everything here was focussed on salt and the region's attraction depended not in its everlasting beauty but on the rich rock-salt mines of Ischl, Hallstatt and Altaussee as well. After its extraction the salt was carried to the salt-works, tarred, and (especially at Gmunden) packed and transported by way of the river. The salt-work administration made sure that all of the local inhabitants were under its employment, turning away all outsiders so that nothing might compromise productivity.

It was thus that this small region - already difficult to reach by its very nature - developed a life of its own. The later additions of the Mondsee, Wolfgangsee and Attersee districts that were also dependent on the salt-works administration did little to alter the area's isolated unity.

Among the regions of the Salzburg Alps, Salzkammergut can be distinguished by its large number of lakes; Salzkammergut ends where the lakes are no longer close to one another. It includes the upper stretch of the Traun River (with all of its lateral valleys) as far as the lower Traunsee at Gmunden and the areas around the Mondsee and the Attersee. In this region - 70 kilometers long and 50 kilometers wide - nature offers everything that can be desired in mountain territory: a glacier, mountains and precipices, pleasant vallies and, above all, a great many lakes. Nearly every mountain is reflected in water, where its image becomes still more enchanting.

The lakes in this area have attracted man since remote times. The earliest prehistoric inhabitants constructed pile-dwellings on their shores or in the water. Later they discovered deposits of salt and - with considerable difficulty - managed to extract it. This brought about a stable existence upon which the extraordinary prehistoric Civilization of Hallstatt was built. Even the Celts and the Romans benefited from the riches of this otherwise inhospitable land, and only after them did things subside until, at the beginning of the 14th century, the salt mines in Hallstatt were opened, marking the beginning of the era of Hapsburgean monopoly in Salzkammergut. This dominion deeply affected the region, and in a decidedly negative way. And yet it is the salt that was indirectly responsable for the development in Salzkammergut of tourism, today the region's most important economical activity. It is certainly unlikely that the area would have gained such popularity if the summer residence of Francis Joseph I had not been established there for over 83 years. However, had it not been for the salt, the emperor would probably never have existed. His parents, unable to have children, underwent a thermal cure at Ischl and shortly afterward Francis Joseph and his three brothers were born. The «prince of salt», duly grateful, dedicated much of his time to Ischl when he became emperor. Here he hunted and celebrated his birthdays and other festivities; here he fell in love, and here he signed the declaration that marked the beginning of the First World War.

But even then it was evident that Salzkammergut was not to be admired for its salt alone. The effects of this «Austrian Switzerland's» scenery were exhilerating to such a degree that for most of the artists and poetically inclined inhabitants of traditional Austria, summer on the lakes became a delightful habit. Important works of art were created here, and at times the landscape took a symbolic leading role in literature, as it often did in the novels by Adalbert Stifter who found inspiration in Salzkammergut. The region is also appreciated for its outstanding architecture: handsome Gothic houses may be found everywhere as well as Baroque churches with fine doors and altars, and innumerable villas in the Neoclassic style. Examples of folk art exist in abundance: crèches with hundreds of figures and with exquisite renderings of the Child; the typical ceramic crockery with its charming spontaneous quality; and folklore that lives on with enduring vitality in its original forms of expression, especially in dance and song. The traditional manner, for example, in which the people of Ebensee or of Bad Aussee celebrate their carnival is still entertaining, and represents a veritable «monument» to Austrian folk culture.

And so it is not surprising that this region, so well loved by its people, should remain in the hearts of its many visitors, above all among those who - rather than following the usual beaten track of the tourist itinerary - have discovered that every corner of Salzkammergut has something novel to offer and have enjoyed human contacts with those remarkable inhabitants who love and defend their traditions. The lakes and mountains, moreover, offer endless opportunities for sports activities. Salzkammergut has been a popular vacation centre since the days of the emperor Francis Joseph up to our time; every year it is visited by the present chancellor of Germany.

The attractions of such a beautiful region shall never be lost or forgotten.

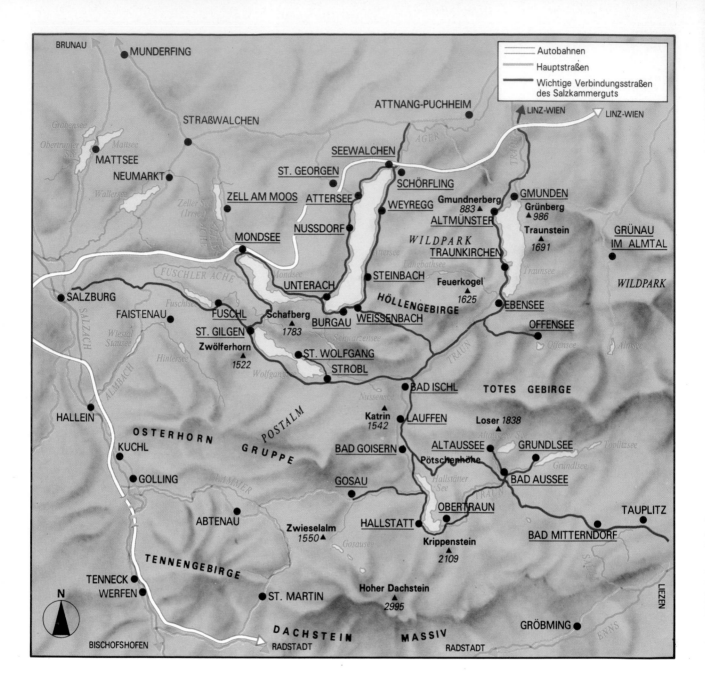

Gmunden seen from the Kalvarienberg.

GMUNDEN

Gmunden has always been the principal centre of Salzkammergut; formerly seat of the salt-works administration, today it is head of the district. It is also the only town to have been surrounded by a wall. During the last century kings and archdukes costructed their castles around the vast inlet of the Traunsee, lending Gmunden an aura of nobility which perfectly suited its magnificent setting on the north shore of the lake. The construction of the handsome **Esplanade** dates from that period. The Stadtplatz, open on one side with a fine vista overlooking the lake, is one of the loveliest squares in the town. On the opposite side we find the **Rathaus** (town hall), elegantly manneristic in form and with a ceramic carillion. In the **Pfarrkirche** (parish church) over the main altar, the *Three Kings* group by Thomas Schwanthaler is particularly interesting.

The town's main attraction is the **Ort castel**, built on a tiny island off the mainland and reached by a long wooden bridge. It enjoyed its heyday around 1880 when it belonged to the archduke Johann Salvator who caused a scandle for his rebellion against the Hapsburg monarchy. After an amourous relationship with a ballerina, and following the loss of his title of nobility, he eventually died in South America. The best view of Gmunden can be had by climbing one of the hills that surround the town - the same romantic town that was once dear to Franz Schubert and Johannes Brahms.

The Ort Castle on a small island in the lake - one of the most romantic scenes in Salzkammergut.

The Stadtplatz of Gmunden with the Renaissance Rathaus on the left and old houses in the background.

The bay af Altmünster, ideal for water sports.

ALTMÜNSTER

The mountains slope gracefully down into the little bay on the north Traunsee, and to the town of Altmünster in its beautiful setting for which it became justly famous during the last century. Here the archdukes of Este settled in the noble old residence of Ebenzweier and the kings of Württemberg built themelves an imposing castle. The locality's history dates back to a great deal earlier however. In a document from the year 909 there is mention of an abbey of Trunseo (the equivalent of Traunsee), and many scholars believe that the name Altmünster (antique monastery) or Münster refers to this early convent. A few architectural remenants such as the church of St. Benedict with its ancient stone tower would seem to bear out the hypothesis. The church contains works of art from several periods, among them the *All Saints Altar* of 1518.

The Traunsee's most temperate waters are found here at Altmünster, where many visitor come for sailing and bathing. Higher up, on the mountains that frame the town, the charming **Hochkreut Park** forest reserve is rich in fauna and has a fine view of the lake. One's eye is irresistibly drawn to the powerful Traunstein whose steep sides plunge directly into the water. Daring footpaths climb to its summit - a breathtaking challenge even to experienced hikers.

The Ebenzweier Castle which belonged to the archdukes of Austria-Este. Franz Schubert sojourned there in 1825.

Views of the splendid Hochkreut Park situated 1,000 meters above Altmünster.

TRAUNKIRCHEN

The southernmost banks of the Traunsee are pressed against such steep rock that parts of the road and the railway run through a tunnel. Until the last century this stretch was totally without communication routes and could be reached only by boat. At the very beginning of this secluded spot, sitting on a little peninsula that juts into the lake, is the ancient village of Traunkirchen. It is said that this peninsula was once a place of cult devoted to pagan gods. Indeed, a stone head eroded by time that probably belonged to the statue of an idol can still be seen in the little church of St. Johann.

The **Paris church** was originally part of a nunnery which according to custom was founded by the dukes after a victorious battle against the pagans. The building now standing however, with its unusual bell towers at either end, belongs to the Baroque period when the monastery was turned over to the Gesuits. The Gesuits added considerable emellishment to the church's interior, including a richly decorated pulpit representing the **Miraculous draught of fishes**. Traunkirchen has many charming sights, but perhaps the most picturesque of them is to be found in its cemetery, with typical wrought iron crosses and a splendid vista over the northern part of the lake as far as Gmunden. This view was

*The romantic enclosure
of the convent at Traunkirchen.*

*Following page:
the Traunstein and the lake.*

"Gisela", the oldest coal-driven paddle-steamer in the world, has been plying the Traunsee since 1872.

A magnificent view of the Traunsee as seen from the cemetery.

already among the more famous ones of Salzkammergut during the Biedermeier period.

At both Traunkirchen and Hallstatt, on *Corpus Domini* holidays the monstrance is carried across the lake in a magnificent procession of boats decorated with flowers and flags.

Finally, the wide beach of Bräuwiese with its little port must not be overlooked; it would be difficult to find another such well-equipped vacation locality in Austria that has shown such respect for its environment. The culture and beauty of Traunkirchen have attracted many artists and musicians including Frans Schubert, Hugo Wolff and Arnold Schonberg.

EBENSEE

The Traun River flows through the entire length of the Traunsee. On the southern extremity of the lake at the point where the Traun enters it is Ebensee, once the industrial centre of Salzkammergut. Large salt-works were already installed in this wooded area in the 17th century. The salt water, that is - the salt solution obtained from the rock salt excavated in the mines, was transported here by way of costly wooden ducts extending over many kilometers, undoubtedly one of the world's oldest pipelines. The old salt-works buildings no longer exist; they were substituted in 1979, a few kilometers farther south of Ebensee, with a modern refinery where 400,000 tons of salt are produced every year.

The funicular railway of the Feuerkogel; in the valley, the little town of Ebensee.

The parish church of Ebensee; in the background the slopes of the Feuerkogel.

The stone lion that commemorates the completion of the Traunkirchen-Ebensee road (1861).

Yet even while other extensive plants are being built, thanks to the love of tradition, Ebensee has not become a grey industrial zone. Its oldest customs, its many-peopled crèches, the bell race at Epiphany and the carnival are all kept alive with enthusiasm.

The city is surrounded by lovely countryside and has, aside from the Traunsee, several smaller lakes (the two Langbathseen lakes and the Offensee) where the emperor Francis Joseph was fond of hunting. The Ebensee panorama is crowned by the Feuerkogel (reached by funicular railway) - a veritable skier's and hiker's paradise at an altitude of about 1,600 meters. It is the last of the mountains before the descent to the plains; on a fine day one can see as far as the Danube and beyond.

To the east we find the Gassl-Tropfsteinhöhle, a splendid grotta filled with ravines and fantastic concretions. The mountain surrounding it is called Schlafende Griechin (Sleeping Greek Girl). The name bears witness to the love of classical antiquities typical of travelers (the acestors of Salzkammergut's modern tourists) who arrived during the romantic period.

Ebensee, on the south shore of the Traunsee.

14

BAD ISCHL

Bad Ischl presents an agreeable picture of a comfortable little Austrian city with several buildings that pre-date the Biedermeier period. Although it was once the summer residence of the emperor and health resort of the Austro-Hungarian monarchy, it is nearly devoid of grand thermal temples and palaces, the only exceptions being the **Kurhaus**, the Palace of the Post, and a few aristocratic hotels of the period. Even in its heyday the city saw that it was useless to attempt to surpass its imposing natural surroundings, so that summer residences were built in the pleasing style adopted for villas which, while fascinating, rarely gave pretence to luxury. The emperor himself gave a good example; indeed, **Kaiservilla** strikes one rather for its impressive setting than for its architecture. It is a typical villa of large terraces and luminous rooms. A simplicity of taste is particularly evident in the more private quarters such as the emperor's bedroom, where the soberly designed bed and washstand share little with the sumptuous furnishings in the princely castles of the day as those occupied by the king of Bavaria Ludwig II. The only unusual note is struck by the large number of trophies on display (the monarch killed over 50,000 animals). The fountain in front of the Kaiservilla is by the Viennese sculptor in vogue at the time - Viktor Tilgner; not far from the fountain is the *Statue of the Dog Trainer*, a gift from the queen of Eng

The exterior of the museum of the city of Bad Ischl.
Today the house in which Emperor Francis Joseph celebrated his engagement to Princess Elisabeth in 1853 contains the collections of the municipal museum of Bad Ischl.

Emperor Francis Joseph as a hunter.
The Emperor loved to go hunting in his summer resort of Bad Ischl. The showcase in the municipal museum in Bad Ischl shows him dressed as a hunter, surrounded by mementos of his sojourn.

DIE PRIESTER DER KIRCHE SOLLEN ÜBER DEN KRANKEN BETEN UND IHN MIT ÖL SALBEN. Jak. 5.14.

EIN GROSSES SAKRAMENT IST DIESES, ICH SAGE, ABER IN CHRISTO U. IN DER KIRCHE. Eph. 5.32.

Statue of the emperor Francis Joseph in hunting dress.

Mosaics in the Pfarrkirche depicting the imperial family. The bearded figure represents Francis Joseph's father; behind him are the emperor and his consort.

The villa of the composer Franz Lehár.

The Kurhaus, where «Operetta Week» is held.

The façade of the Kaiservilla.

The fountain in front of the Kaiservilla.
On the right, the Statue of the
Dog Trainer is visible.

land. The nearby pavilion of the
emperess Elizabeth («Sissi»), the
Marmorschlössel, emanates the
romantic mystery of the lady who
ordered its construction. Today the
Marmorschlössel houses the interesting *Photographic Museum of
Upper Austria*.
The emperor's sojourns at Ischl are
commemorated in various monu-
ments. The most notable of these is
to be found in a secluded place
about three kilometers from town
at the foot of a cliff. The statue is
known as the *Kaiser-Jagd-
Standbild* and depicts the sovereign
in hunting dress, while a horned
stag that he has just killed lies at his
feet. The villa faces the Wolfgang-

The stairway of the Kaiservilla.

Part of the collection in the Kaiservilla of over 50,000 hunting trophies.

An old photograph of the emperor's father Francis Charles riding through the park on a sedan-chair.

tal where Francis Joseph enjoyed taking morning walks during his later years. The actress Katharina Schratt also lived in the villa.

Artists and musicians and political personalities who spent their summers here are also commemorated, among them Johannes Brahms, Anton Bruckner, Johann Strauss and above all Franz Lehár who established his residence at Ischl and remained until his death. His villa is open to the public.

Every summer many internationally famed actors and singers appeared at the old theatre of Ischl, a meeting-place for Hapsburgean high-society. It has since been converted for cinema and named the «Franz Lehár Film Theatre».

The spring-water of Bad Ischl is still very much appreciated for its therapeutic qualities. It may be drunk in the neoclassic **Trinkhalle** built in 1831, or in the **Kurmittelhaaus**, built by Clemens Holzmeister in 1932, to which a modern Hydrothermal indoor pool has been annexed. The famous «Operetta Weeks» (Operettenwochen) and other mundane events are held in the Kurhaus.

The city's surroundings are of course among its major attractions, for few alpine areas have as many walks and excursions to offer. At the limits of the district territory is a picturesque mountain lake, the Nussensee, and Mount Katrin (served by the funicular railway and with a fine view), popular for its ski runs. Paths in every direction lead to pastures, gorges or summits - more than can be explored in one visit.

The Kaiservilla's Red Room.

Francis Joseph's bed.

Francis Joseph's study.

The Marmorschlössel, preferred residence of the emperor at Ischl, and now a photography museum.

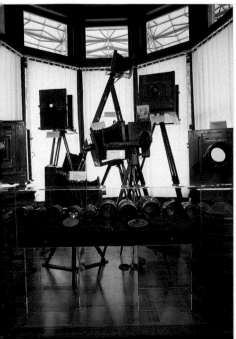

Lauffen, the old marketplace.
In the foreground, the river Lauffen.

The old houses of Lauffen.

LAUFFEN

Lauffen, the old market town, is situated a few kilometers above Bad Ischl where the valley narrows. Here the Traun River plunges in the so-called «Wilder Lauffen» waterfall, once a dangerous obstacle for salt transportation by river. It is doubtful that a town would have grown up on such an unlikely site had it not been for the labour employed for the manouvering and maintaining of the locks and other dam operations. The church with its imposing bell tower is a famous sanctuary.

BAD GOISERN

After the narrow valley of Lauffen the mountains separate and give way to the long sunny valley where Bad Goisern stands. According to legend on this site there was once a city governed by a king named Goisaram who acquired great wealth from the riches of the mountains. The settlement may well be very old, as up until the 16th century Goisern was the head parish for all of Salzkammergut. Solid old houses, mills and hotels still make up a harmonious urban picture. Two thirds of the population uphold the evangelical faith, as testified by two churches. Protestantism has tenaciously resisted throughout the centuries among the comunities of Salzkammergut, especially among the timber and salt-workers. In 1880 Goisern became a spa locality after the discovery of an iodic sulfide spring.

The loveliest scenic spots occur along the slopes surrounding the valley. One encounters enchanting pastures such as the Hütteneckalm,

The old houses of Bad Goisern.

whose vista was already immortalized in a famous painting by Ferdinand Waldmüller around 1830. A callanging but entirely safe trail along the Ewige Wand (eternal wand) - a gigantic rock face - offers a marvelous view over the Goisern Valley. Across the valley a forest road leads to the **Chorinsky Lock**, an old and picturesque river dam constructed to facilitate timber transportation.

The district of Bad Goisern includes a part of the Hallstättersee valley, situated on the sunny northern shore of this otherwise rather melancholy lake. At the point where the lower lake narrows into the Traun, once an important station for transporting salt by river, the old buildings are still standing.

The lovely pastures of the area surrounding Bad Goisern.

The point where the Hallstättersee spills into the Traun River, and the old Steeg Tavern.

The old Chorinsky lock that aided
transportation of logs along the river.

The daring path along the so-called
«Ewige Wand» or «eternal wall», which
affords the climber a fine view.

GOSAU

A long and incaccessable gorge on one side and an almost 1,000 meter Alpine pass on the other nearly cut Gosau off from the rest of the world. The isolation of this quiet valley has allowed it to conserve much of its original character. The houses are built mostly of wood, and - an unusual circumstance in Austria - more than 85% of the inhabitants are of the evangelican faith (the town has two churches). Gosau is also one of the best skiing areas in all of Salzkammergut.

The valley opens onto the Vordere Gosausee. Here, where the immense rock face and the glaciers of the Dachstein are mirrored into the blue waters of the lake, the majesty of the Alps seems particularly impressive. A funicular railway climbs to the Zwieselam which offers, if possible, a still more fascinating view of the Dachstein. The wild and serrated profile of its peak deeply impresses one with a mixture of aversion and of challenging attraction.

The Dachstein is the easternmost mountain of the Alps and is the pride of the Upper Austrian and Styrian provinces. It is just a few meters short of 3000, reaching a height of 2,996.

The peaceful fields of Gosau.

The Gosausee with the massive Dachstein in the background.

HALLSTATT

Hallstatt is probably the most fascinating spot in the Alps. Imagine a little town clinging to the side of an enormous mountain, in a position seldom reached by sun during the winter. The houses are mostly old and huddled together, with picturesque little streets and squares. The name Hallstatt originates from one of the most famous prehistoric civilizations - an unexpected heritage to find in such an isolated location, to which its interesting Baroque and medieval works of art may be added. But simplicity predominates. A glimpse at the pace of life outside the tourist season and one is struck by the mystery of the place.

To reach the site where salt has been extracted from the mountain from the time of the prehistoric settlers, one takes the funicular railway to the famous Gräberfeld, where the greater part of the Hallstatt Civilization's remains have been uncovered. One may also visit the oldest rock-salt mine in the world at Salzbergwerk, and continue the descent on foot to Hallstatt by following the steep route of the salt water duct. An absolute must is the **museum**, for a glimpse at an era when Hallstatt was «richer than Rome». Some unusual exhibits include a rucksack from 2,500 years ago. Unfortunately the ancient miner conserved in salt is not among them; he was discovered in 1734 - but as he had been a pagan, he was unceremoniously buried in unconsecrated soil.

The late Gothic church above the town is also worth visiting. It contains frescoes, and outstanding paneled altars of 1450 and 1520.

The church and houses of Hallstatt situated along the lake's narrow shores.

The houses of Hallstatt
clinging to the mountain.

The triangular Marktplatz
with the Trinity Column.

The «Saltworks Band».

The typical boat of the
Salzkammergut lakes, called
«Traunerl» or « Plätte ».

Facing page:
The old «Stockerhaus»,
location of the Heimatmuseum.

Objects on display in the Prehistoric
Museum. From left to right:
a beaked pitcher, an oil container,
a dagger.

Next to the chuch is the famous **Ossuary of Hallstatt** (Beinhouse) in which 1,200 skulls and countless human bones of rather small dimensions are gathered. After a brief repose in the local cemetery the bones were transferred to the ossuary; each skull bears the painted initials of the deceased and the symbols that represented the cause of death.

At the town's centre - which would probably have a very different aspect today had the oldest parts not been destroyed by a memorable fire in 1750 - is the little triangular Marktplatz with the Baroque *Trinity Column*. A backdrop of sheer rock face and a high waterfall behind the square lend it a special enchantment. The main road passes the town by through two long tunnels, leaving the streets of Hallstatt free of automobiles.

The best excursion departing from Hallstatt leads to Kalvarienberg, where there is an excellent view. Chapels dedicated to the various **stations of the cross** contain images of Christ's Passion. After reaching the summit of the Kalvarienberg the path descends to the Echerntal Valley which terminates with the magnificent Strub Falls. This awesome setting, which goes by the name of «Waldbachstrub», is one of the favorite subjects of landscape painters.

Thanks to a newly made pathway it is now possible to walk all the way around the lake. Excursions can al-

Portal of the church with frescoes and memorial tablets.

The Ossuary, in which 1,200 skulls and countless bones are heaped.

so be taken on the Dachstein, whose high and dark rock face looms over the southern shore of the Hallerstättersee.

When the German writer Wilhelm Raabe (1831-1910) arrived for the first time at Hallstatt, he asked the inn keeper what sights he might visit should there be bad weather. The answer greatly amused the writer, who made a note of it with his own comment: « 'Hallstatt' replied the inn keeper, and he was quite right - three times right ». « 'Hallstatt', he said, 'is an extraordinary place in any weather' » (from the guidebook of Salzkammergut by Karl Pilz).

The main altar by Leonhard Astl (1520).

The small altar (1450), whose panels were stolen.

Detail of the small paneled altar.

OBERTRAUN

Obertraun is situated in the valley below the Dachstein. From here a funicular railway climbs the Krippenstein to a vast calcarious plateau, offering an unusual experience to skiers as well as to hikers. The area is famous for its caverns (**Höhlen**). Towards the valley is the Koppenbrüllerhöhle, crossed by a wide stream and situated at an altitude of about 1350 meters, and the Eishöhle and the Mammuthöhle, both of which may be reached by funicular railway. It is superfluous to remark that the sight of this subterranean world leaves a strong and unforgettable impression. The caverns accessible to tourists make up only a small part of the Dachstein network - which includes at least two hundred of them.

The point where the Koppenbrüllerhöhle's subterranean stream emerges.

The interior of the Riesen-eishöle. (Photo: Fotoverlag Scheurecker, Schärding)

GRUNDLSEE

The Grundlsee belongs to the Styrian Salzkammergut region. It is remarkable - rather than for the town of that name situated on the northern shore (and summer residence of several eminent personalities in the world of economics and art) - for the splendid lake that extends from east to west over 6 kilometers at the foot of the Totes Gebirge. Its entire shore is suitable for bathing.

The road stops at the lake's western end. After a walk of about a half hour towards the rock face a quiet little lake immersed in the solitude of the woods appears - the Toplitzsee - famous for the Nazi treasures

The eastern part of the Grundlsee.

The still unspoiled shores of the Grundlsee.

The Toplitzsee, shrouded in mystery.

Details of the charming wooden houses typical of the area around the Aussee.

that are said to lie at the bottom. Having crossed the lake by boat, one comes upon the most enchanting spot of the excursion - the little Kammersee. The source of the Traun River is here in the heart of the mountain.

The Grundlsee was the scene of the Archduke Johann's love for «Nani», the postmaster's daughter who later became his wife.

BAD AUSSEE

Ausseerland - a valley with numerous lakes and an extremely varried landscape - has belonged to the province of Styria since remote times, as opposed to the rest of Salzkammergut which belongs, almost in its entirety, to Upper Austria. At Aussee, the natural centre of this region, administrative offices and installations similar to those at Gmunden were established for the extracting of salt. The area therefore has many old buildings, as well as a home for elderly and ill salt labourers constructed in the 14th century. The

The old church of St. Leonhard.

The Parish Church St. Peter.

The covered swimming pool in the modern spa complex.

Chapel of this institution is the jewel of Ausseerland, and contains two paneled altars, frescoes, and antique sculptures.

The **Leonhardtkirche** up on the hill is almost equally as lovely and has a sequence of Gothic panel paintings. A little **museum** exhibits interesting information on the history of salt extraction.

The house where the local postmaster's daughter Anna Plochl was born stands in the market place. Despite opposition from the Viennese court she married the emperor Francis Joseph's brother, the arch-

View of the Bad Aussee Valley;
on the left is the Loser.

The Alpine garden at Bad Aussee.

duke Johann, and shared a long and happy existence with him. Other spots are reminiscent of Ausseerland's renowned guests, such as the composers Wilhelm Kienzel and Richard Strauss, and writers such as Arthur Schnitzler. But Bad Aussee offers a great deal more than its cultural attractions. For guests who wish to undergo the salt water cure, a modern spa with indoor pool has been constructed. There are countless walks and excursions. And a sojourn here should certainly be completed with a climb up the Loser, which dominates the landscape with its rocky fortress-like structure. The excursions may be made in automobile on the panoramic road up to an altitude of 1,600 meters; about an hour's walk leads to the summit and an incomparable vista. The Loser is also considered to be one of the best skiing spots of Styria.

An interesting and unusual feature of Ausseerland is its Alpine garden (Alpengarten) created in 1914 and containing 4,000 species of Alpine plants. From here one may continue on to the Sommerbergersee, a little lake with temperate waters suitable for bathing, and surrounded by woods and marshes.

The marvelous vista over the Altausseersee from the Loser.

The rocky peak of the Loser.

Houses in the region around the Altausseersee, usually built in wood.

ALTAUSSEE

Of all of the Salzkammergut lakes, the Altaussee is perhaps the most beautiful. There are days when this lake has an almost irrealistic charm, despite the looming rocks that surround it and the eternal glaciers of the Dachstein visible in the distance. It is not surprising that this place was frequented by writers such as Hugo von Hofmannstahl or Fredrich Torberg. The lake is often compared humorously to a gigantic inkwell in which poets dipped their pens to set their best verses to paper.

View of the Altausseersee, surrounded by sheer rock.

A little beach, with the Dachstein rising in the distance.

STROBL

Strobl, unlike the other towns of the Wolfgangsee, has always maintained the characteristics of a snug little farming village nestled between lake and mountain. Yet in recent years the inhabitants have made an effort to offer visitors the same attractions that can be found in the other two vacation centres of the Wolfgangsee - and have succeeded without compromising the intimate atmosphere for which Strobl is particularly appreciated. An especially pleasant feature is its position on a little sunlit bay facing

View of Strobl from the Bürglstein trail.

Another view of Strobl, famous for its water skiing.

west with an animated lakefront and an excellent beach. Several famous actors have lived at Strobl, including Theo Lingen (who was also mayor of the town) and Emil Jannings.

The trail around the Bürglstein and the Postalm road have been carried out during the last few decades. The trail winds through the Bürglstein rocks that overhang the lake with vistas of the Wolfgangsee and its surroundings. This is one of the most pleasurable and spectacular walks of Salzkammergut.

The Postalm road climbs to an altitude of 1,200 meters - to the second largest pasture area of the Eastern Alps. One is struck not only by the road itself that climbs the steep valley of the Weiss Stream, but especially by the vast plateau that affords exceptional Alpine views in every direction, easy excursions, and winter skiing facilities (several skilifts and one of the best ski runs in Europe).

The Bürglstein, whose wooded slopes reach the water.

Tourist and sports facilities at Strobl.

The lakefront of Strobl with its sweeping view as far as St. Wolfgang.

Sunset on the Wolfgangsee.

Two Alpine scenes of the Postalm.

When spring comes,
when the snow melts,
I return to the Alpine pastures.

With the cows and their softly
ringing bells,
with my young bull,
with the calfs
and with the tender little lambs.

(folk song)

ST. WOLFGANG

Few lakeside resorts are as fortunate as St. Wolfgang on the Wolfgangsee. The eye is gratified in every season with the beauty of the lake and its alternating shores of cliffs, woods, and soft meadows, compassed by mountains that create a harmoniously pleasing picture on every side - some rough and steep at their summits, others rounded. These offer a great variety of excursions in the lake area. The lake itself provides year-around sports enjoyment: bathing and windsurf in its tepid waters during the summer months, and ice skating in the winter.

In addition to its unique natural virtues, St. Wolfgang possesses admirable works of art. Besides being an important centre for summer Alpine vacationing, it was for centuries the destination of pilgrims from all over Europe. The church's foundation is attributed to St. Wolfgang who was bishop of Ratisbona from 972 to 994 and who, according to legend, lived as a hermit on the Falkenstein in a rude setting high above the western shore of the lake. He slept in grottoes and quenched his thirst with the spring-water that he himself had caused to flow from the rock. But the devil tormented him, and so that his temptations might cease he is said to have thrown his axe down from the mountain with a vow to build a church on the spot where it fell. He found it far off where the town of St. Wolfgang stands today. There he built his

View of the Wolfgangsee.

A picturesque view of St. Wolfgang from the lake.

The lakefront of St. Wolfgang.

The harmonious mountain chain that encircles the lake.

church, and legend has it that he made the devil his servant. Eventually he returned to Ratisbona, but first he promised to effect a great many miracles on the scene of his former hermitage. It was thus that so many pilgrims rushed there and St. Wolfgang became known throughout the world. Markings in the rock and other traces of his saintly life can still be seen. Even the trail up the Falkenstein has its moments of compelling enchantment.

St. Wolfgang was particularly venerated in the church bearing his name, which is rich in works of art. It contains a *paneled altar* mounted in gold by the Tyrolese artist Michael Pacher, finished in 1481.

Its central figures in *intaglio* represent mediaval man's vision of Heaven, where God and the saints sit majestically on their thrones in blessedness. This group is framed by 16 large panel paintings and 4 small ones - very fine in structure, in masterly painting and in attention to detail. The church also has works of Baroque art such as the large *double altarpiece* by Thomas Schwanthaler and an expressive statue by Meinrad Guggenbichler, a native of Mondsee.

The legend of St. Wolfgang and the devil is reproduced in a charming chapel built near the place of the saint's hermitage. An arched portico and a *fountain* (1515) complete the sanctuary.

From this portico one can see - directly below the chapel - the famous hotel «Zum Weissen Rossl» (the White Horse Inn) and its beach. From the markplatz, an archway through an ivy-covered house leads to the street dominated by the hotel - with its door that opens onto Prosperity, according to the operetta that has made the Wolfgangsee popular the world over with its merry songs.

St. Wolfgang has a third attraction: the Schafberg with its rack-rail train. This mountain commands a particularly impressive panorama. Its northern face drops abruptly to the valley forming a sort of pulpit at its summit from which the Mondsee appears directly below. Farther beyond, a dozen other lakes, as well as the mountains as far as the Alti Tauri and

The old pilgrim's fountain in front of the church.

Summer vacationing at St. Wolfgang.

Traditional costumes of St. Wolfgang.

Summer shopping in St. Wolfgang.

their glaciers are visible. The Schafberg was so popular at the beginning of the 19th century that a carrying service was arranged to take visitors up who were unable to manage the climb on foot. The rack-rail train was completed in just two years (1892-1893) and is still operating, with a record of no accidents to its credit although it carries over 200,000 passengers every year. The town of St. Wolfgang, despite its considerable modernization, is pleasant and hospitable. The inhabitants - solicitous of their guests - have kept up a high standard of gastronomy in their restaurants and a **Doll Museum** had been founded by private enterprise.

Portico in front of the church.

Interior of the church of St. Wolfgang.

The altar by Michael Pacher.

The Marktplatz of St. Wolfgang; on the right, the arch that leads to the «White Horse Inn».

The «White Horse Inn».

The hotel's sign - that has become world famous through the operetta of the same name.

The Schafberg, where the shephards of St. Wolfgang still graze their sheep («Schafe» in German).

The upper station of the Schafberg's rack-railway and the hotel at the top.

The nearly 100 year old rack-railway.

As throughout the rest of Salzkammergut, the most effective way to be in tune with the local people is to take part in their festivities, where antique costumes are worn with fine gilt caps and where the well-known dirndl is always present. Every town is equipped with its own brass band, and many play folk music for their own enjoyment without ever making a public appearance. *Leider*, *jodler*, and the typical dances are, for the people of Salzkammergut, the symbol of their country and their independence.

The Wolfgangsee seen from the top of the Schafberg.

SCHAFBERG

The mountain was already renowned in the 19th century, and an incomparable view can be enjoyed from its top. The following is a description from a guidebook of 1910.

"The Schafberg is especially famous for its vista which is practically unrivaled in magnificence and quite unique in some respects. Fourteen lakes are visible from the top; the view across the plain extends beyond the Danube as far as Southern Bohemia while mountains stretch out into the distance like a sea of rock. At the foot of the Schafberg's steep wall lie the Alpine valleys of Eisenau and Acker, while directly beneath us are the ripples of the Mondsee and the Attersee. A heart unmoved by so much beauty is surely to be pittied, as it cannot know nature's great book, nor penetrate the marvels concealed in it".

View of the Attersee from the Schafberg.

The Himmelspfortenhütte refuge on the Schafberg and below, the Mondsee.

View of St. Gilgen and the Wolfgangsee.

ST. GILGEN

St. Gilgen, Strobl, and Fuschl belong to the Salzburgese region of Salzkammergut. At St. Gilgen (named for St. Giles, the patron saint of the church) the archbishops established the seat of the region. Their administrators were called curates and lived in a building facing the lake - now the courthouse. In 1720 the curate's daughter Anna Pertl - who was to marry the musician Leopold Mozart and become mother of the great Wolfgang Amadeus - was born in this house. A fountain in the centre of S. Gilgen commemorates the composer.

St. Gilgen is not made up of the tight rows of houses typical of the old market towns but has many distinguished buildings such as the **Rathaus** (which has an interesting collection of hunting trophies) and the hotel «Zur Post», decorated with 17th century frescoes.

St. Gilgen's nearest mountain is the Zwolferhorn, which has a view almost as beautiful as the one from the Schafberg and a famous and challenging ski run. The excursions in this area lead to pastures and to spots where one finds oneself in almost complete solitude.

Recently St. Gilgen has become famous as the vacation resort of Germany's chancellor Helmut Kohl, though it has long been the traditional summer residence of important artists and scientists. Among these were the great physician Theodor Billroth and the Nobel Prizewinner Karl von Frisch. The picturesque group of houses that belonged to the Frisch family, the so-called «**Brunnwinkel**», is considered to be among the most charming corners of Salzkammergut. A pathway circling the lake leads to Fürberg at the foot of Mount Falkenstein, once the Mecca of pilgrims.

There are many places for bathing and water sports; there are vast meadows, woods that extend down to the water, steep banks, tiny inlets, and, on the rocks that emerge from the water - numerous crosses in memory of legendary events (the «Wedding Cross», the «Cross of the Ox» and others).

16th century frescoes on the façade of the hotel «Zur Post».

The Rathaus of St. Gilgen. In the background, the church's handsome bell tower.

The Mozart fountain that commemorates the birth of the composer's mother in St. Gilgen.

In Salzkammergut one can
be merry
when the music plays.
Holldrioh!

The elder may flower
all through summer.

It's only love that
flowers all the year.

In Salzkammergut one can
be merry
when the music plays.
Holldrioh!

From the operetta
"The White Horse Inn"

*Brunnwinkel, summer residence
of the Nobel Prize-winner
Karl von Frisch.*

*A group of sailboats at St. Gilgen,
where sailing is very popular.*

The Castle of Fuschl.

FUSCHL

The Fuschlsee is located at the western extremity of Salzkammergut. Its shores are still free of buildings and are in many places ideal for bathing. On the right bank stands Fuschl, with its handsome lakefront and beach.

The most important architectural feature of the area is the Schloss Fuschl, a castle situated a few kilometers outside the town on a narrow strip of land. It once served the archbishops of Salzburg as a hunting lodge, and has since become a delux hotel frequented by persons from the world of politics and finance. A restaurant and a hunting museum have been ac-comodated in an inn which was part of the old castle complex. The surrounding game reserve testifies to the area's importance as a hunting spot, not to mention the opportunuties for fishing in a lake well provided with fish. Above the little town of Fuschl are the ruins of Wartenfel where a fine view overlooks the hills that flatten gradually out as they approach the valley.

THE MONDSEE

The prettiest and most temperate lake of the region is the Mondsee which has co-existed with mankind since remote times. Here our ancestors constructed lake-dwellings (later termed pile-dwellings or *palafitte*) on wooden poles. This took place during the Neolithic epoch - a phase of man's development which has become symbolic of early civilization. The shores were probably also inhabited by the Romans; the gigantic abbey, founded by the dukes of Bavaria in 748, was built over Roman ruins. For over one thousand years the abbey influenced the art of its region - from the times of Romanesque art when illuminations that could compete with the highest European standards were painted; during the period of Gothic art when the big churches of abbeys and other important edifices were built, to the Baroque period when the sculptor Meinrad Guggenbichler, the «Master of Mondsee», was commissioned to embellish most of the churches in the area with his fine works.

Thus the Mondsee region - though it remained quite isolated until only a few years ago - possesses a significant artistic heritage. A visit to the church of the abbey, the second oldest church of Upper Austria with a magnificent main altar and sculptures by Guggenbichler, should not be missed.

The folk art has also been preserved, and may be admired in the **Heimatmuseum** and especially in the **Rauchhouse** - an early type of farmhouse (a similar one situated above the market has been set up as a museum).

As with every resort town in Salzkammergut Mondsee has also had its distinguished visitors, including the Sweedish writer August Strinberg. In the environs we find places of exceptional beauty: the big Zellersee with its shores for the most part still intact, and the vast peat-bog on the Mondseeberg. Charming Baroque churches and chaples are spread throughout the area.

Mondsee is also an up-to-date summer tourist resort, ideal for water sports and famous as the gastronomic centre of Salzkammergut. Thanks to its link with the turnpike, this land of abbeys - once remote - has become a favorite with visitors from all over the world.

"The Mondsee with its distant horizons, the inexplicably sweet aura of peace on the brilliant green high fields with the quiet charm of the magic flow of the glowing lake, with the splendour and diversity of its clusters of rocks, is different from anything else, and perhaps even more moving."
(Helmine von Chezy, 1833)

The facade of the Sfiftskirche (abbey church) of Mondsee.

The main altar of the Sfiftskirche of Mondsee.

The «Kreuzstein» (stone cross) to the west of Mondsee.

View of the Mondsee, with the Schafberg on the right in the background.

THE ATTERSEE

The Attersee is 20 kilometers long and is the largest lake of Salzkammergut. A sheer drop of rock appears at the southern end forming a gorge - the Burgauklamm - but otherwise the countryside is open with softly rolling hills. Several little towns face on the lake, none of them spectacular - but all tidy and inviting. From the surrounding hights one can admire the lake whose apparent uniformity reveals its subtle variations on closer ex-

Promenade along the Attersee.

Unterach, toward the south of the Attersee.

The wild and romantic Burgauklamm.

amination. When the sky is clear the colors of the water change continually with the sun's progress. The atmosphere changes with the different winds, as with the Rosenwind, the favorite for sail-boating. The Attersee's landscape is one for connoisseurs, for those who abandon themselves to nature's most intimate charms. Indeed this immensely beautiful region, with a final glance that scans the vast surface of the lake and the uninterrupted mountain chain - one might well conclude one's visit to Salzkammergut.

*The solitary little church
of Steinbach am Attersee.*

*Summer at the Attersee.
Left: the Kammer castle.*

Evening at the Attersee.

TOURIST INFORMATION FOR A SUMMER SOJOURN
IN THE SALZKAMMERGUT DISTRICT

Mountain roads traversable without difficulty

Gmundnerbergstrasse (883 meters): from the town of Altmünster; fine view; recommended hotel, the «Urz'n».

Postalmstrasse (from 1200 to 1900 meters): toll road climbing from Strobl along the valley of the Weiss Stream. Splendid pastures with many opportunities for excursions and walks.

Neidergadenstrasse (ca. 900 meters): from the Wolfgangsee state highway (south shore of the lake directly in front of St. Wolfgang). A toll road leading to unspoiled pastures. Suitable area for easy alpine excursions (the Bleckwand exursion is recommended).

Halleralmstrasse (ca. 800 metres): from St. Agatha, south of Bad Goisern. A narrow road leading to the Halleralm hotel-refuge. Fine view of the Dachstein.

Loserstrasse (1600 meters): from Altaussee. Road with a very fine view that climbs to just 200 meters beneath the peak of the Loser.

Installations

Grünberg (987 meters): funicular railway from Gmunden. Fine view of the lake and of the Traunstein.

Feuerkogel (1625 meters): funicular railway from Ebensee. Good excursion area unfortunately disfigured by ski runs.

Katrin (1393 meters): funicular railway from Bad Ischl. Magnificent setting at the meeting point of two valleys (the Trauntal and the Wolfgangtal).

Schafberg (1783 meters): rack-railway. Famous observation point overlooking much of Upper Austria.

Zwölferhorn (1522 meters): funicular railway from St. Gilgen. Splendid view of Wolfgangsee.

Dachstein: three funicular railways climb this immense massif -
a) Zwieselalm (1500 meters): from Gosausee (magnificent view)
b) Krippenstein (2100 meters); from Obertraun (near the intermediate station are the famous Dachsteinhöhlen.
c) Schaldminger Gletscher (2613 meters): from Ramsau, on the southern slope of the Dachstein (presence of ice).

Unforgettable walks and excursions

Around the Traunstein: from Gmunden the funicular railway climbs the Grünberg, skirts the solitary Laudachsee and, passing behind the Traunstein (immunity to dizzy hights is necessary), descends at the Traunsee (5 hours).

Zellerlweg to Traunkirchen: the ascent begins at Kalvarienberg (fine view), then fol-

lows a shaded path to the Burgstein Hotel (1 hour); return along the same route.

Falkensteinweg, from St. Gilgen to St. Wolfgang: the trail winds along the steep banks of the lake, then crosses an elevation of about 150 meters, the site of numerous legendary cliffs and chapels (3 hours).

Salzbergweg to Hallstatt: a funicular railway climbs to Salzberg where an ancient path proceedes across the steep mountain slopes and finally descends along the salt water duct to Hallstatt (3 - 4 hours).

Around the Altausseersee: marvelous and still little-known mountain scenery; opportunity for lake-bathing (2 hours).

More difficult excursions
(suitable dress and footwear are necessary)

Traunstein (1693 meters): winding and rocky footpath, very fatiguing. A reasonable amount of mountain climbing experience is required (ascent in about 3 and a half hours).

Schafberg-Seenweg: from the summit of the Schafberg (1783 meters, reached by rack-rail train) the route crosses the Himmelspforte and descends along a rocky footpath (immunity to dizzy hights is necessary) with a view overlooking three lakes; from the vicinity of the Mönichsee the descent continues towards St. Wolfgang (about 4 hours).

Grosser Donnerkogel: from the Zwieselalm (funicular railway), a slightly fatiguing footpath reaches the Donnerkogel (2054 meters) in a rocky area filled with crevaces (about 2 hours).

Heilbronnerkreuz: from the station above the funicular railway of the Krippenstein, a footpath crosses a wide karst plateau covered with mugho pines and leads to a cross in commemoration of a group of pupils who perished from the cold in 1954 (round trip about 4 hours).

Loser: from the end of the mountain road there is about a 2 hour climb to the Loser (1836 meters). Along the way: the little Augstsee, the rocky slopes of the Loserfenster and peak of the Hochanger (a total of about 2 and a half hours).

If it rains

Three rock-salt mines (Bad Ischl, Hallstatt, Altaussee) with guided tours.

Dachsteinhöhlen (grottoes of the Dachstein): Koppenbrüllerhöhle at the bottom of the valley near Obertraun, and Rieseneishöhle and Mammuthöhle near the Krippenstein funicular railway's intermediate station.

Kaiservilla (Imperial Villa) at Bad Ischl, with the Marmorschlössel (a pavilion that houses the museum of photography).

Interesting museums may be found at:

Mondsee (pile-dwellings, works of art from the abbey of Mondsee); Gmunden (ceramics, the history of salt); Hallstatt (prehistoric exhibits); Bad Aussee (rock-salt exhibits); Bad Goisern (the Anzenaumühle outdoor museum).

Indoor swimmign pools: hydrothermal indoor pools at Bad Ischl and Bad Aussee; normal indoor pools at Ebensee, St. Gilgen, Gosau, and Vöcklabruck (about 28 km. from Gmunden).

Places and landmarks of interest in the environs: Salzburg; Berchtesgaden; the Baroque abbey of Kremsmünster (turnpike towards Vienna, exit Sattledt); St. Florian (turnpike towards Vienna, exit St. Florian); Wilhering (on the Danube, a few kilometers above Linz).

Events

During the summer every town and village in Salzkammergut offers its guests some form of entertainment such as folkloristic evenings, band concerts, etc. Especially noteworthy are the narcissus festival in the Bad Aussee district (end of May), the big lake festivals or *Seefeste*, particularly in the towns on the Traunsee, and the unusual festivals of Bad Goisern (among these the so-called «chamois' beard olympics»). The *Corpus Domini* processions at Traunkirchen and Hallstatt are magnificent, as well as the celebration of Emperor Francis Joseph's birthday on August 18th in Bad Ischl.

Water sports

Sailing, windsurf, waterskiing on all of the large lakes; the especially well-equipped bathing resorts include Gmunden, Altmünster (heliotherapy), Mondsee, Fuschl and most of the towns surrounding the Attersee; charming natural beaches at Traunkirchen (Bräuwiese), at St. Gilgen-Fürberg, and on the Langbathsee (near Ebensee), Fuschlsee, Grundlsee and Altrausseersee lakes.

Famous Hotels

Gasthof Grünberg at Gmunden (on the road that climbs the Traunstein; magnificent garden; it overlooks the lake).

Weisses Rössl («The White Horse Inn») at St. Wolfgang (made famous the world over by the operetta of the same name; splendid terrace overlooking the Wolfgangsee).

Plomberg at Mondsee (excellent restaurant).

Häupl at Seewalchen am Attersee (famed restaurant).

Neue Post at Bad Mitterndorf (typical local cuisine).

Café Grellinger at Gmunden (very old and famous café on the Esplanade).

Café Zauner at Bad Ischl (the traditional meeting-place at the time of the «imperial city»).

Café Frauenschuh at Mondsee (typical Austrian café).